salmonpoetry40

Publishing Irish & International

Poetry Since 1981

Dead Reckoning *is a collection of high and beautiful seriousness, containing work of exceptional ambition and achievement. Philosophical, unafraid of the big questions ('And yet why am I here, / father, if I cannot enter?'), Jude Nutter is a poet both well-travelled and well read. Here are poems of collapse and Holocaust, of young love in the Eighties and of love at the end of its long human cycle, all written with an exceptional, cosmopolitan command of language and material. It is part of the very precise genius of this work that Nutter explains how we are each given a body, a buthker, a box, by which we may test and measure our being-in-the-world. In one stunning poem, 'The Shipping Forecast,' this generalised box is metamorphised into a specific love-box from which her father removes a ring to place upon the finger of his comatose and dying wife. All of Nutter's work, no matter how seemingly well-travelled, returns to that inner human circle of love, family memoir and attachment. 'How is it we can be loved / so well and remain so famished still?' she asks in 'Disco Jesus and the Wavering Virgins in Berlin, 2011.' This collection, elegant in thought and technique, attempts to answer that question. Jude Nutter has created a work of great beauty, one of the loveliest collections of the poetry year.*

—THOMAS MCCARTHY author of *Prophecy*, *Pandemonium* and eight other collections

In Dead Reckoning, *Jude Nutter has given us a book of revelation, poems that press wisdom through language, extracting language itself from the dark earth of the body. Beginning in elegy, and ranging across Europe, she unflinchingly opens doors of our deep mortality: natural history and the fossils that move us and human histories of cave paintings, of the Romans, and especially of World War II and the dead of Bergen-Belsen, where the child-poet once lived. By images at once corporeal and luminous, Nutter's reckonings render narrative, reflection, and beauty as inseparable. This gorgeous collection becomes a guide for how to love the dead beyond memory, a book to be returned to again and again.*

—CHRISTINA HUTCHINS author of *Tender the Maker* and *The Stranger Dissolves*

There are lines of surpassing beauty in every one of these poems. Jude Nutter manages the exacting task of writing long while never losing focus on the parts that minutely build up the texture of the whole. She is at once deeply psychological and physical, wielding a naturalist's vocabulary for our common world made strange by our attention to it. When she describes "the quick veer, the glint-thrill, the solid, flexed silm" of a caught trout, we know we are hearing a master of sound. Underneath the elegies in this book is a frighteningly percipient, alert young girl who does not forget the cruelties of private and public history. Dead Reckoning *is a stunning reclamation of that girl and her capacity for love.*

—THOMAS R. SMITH author of *The Glory* and *Windy Day at Kabekona*

Dead Reckoning
Jude Nutter

Published in 2021 by
Salmon Poetry
Cliffs of Moher, County Clare, Ireland
Website: www.salmonpoetry.com
Email: info@salmonpoetry.com

ISBN 978-1-912561-89-6

Cover Artwork: *Cliodhna Cussen: Saint Brendan the Navigator, Brandon Creek, County Kerry, Ireland*
Cover Design & Typesetting: *Siobhán Hutson*

Printed in Ireland by Sprint Print

*Salmon Poetry gratefully acknowledges the support of
The Arts Council / An Chomhairle Ealaíon*

for

E.D.J. 1926–2009

D.N. 1924–2014

Acknowledgements

Grateful acknowledgement is made to the editors of the following journals in which many of these poems, some in earlier versions, first appeared:

American Literary Review: "The Lovers in Bergen–Belsen, 2010"

Arts and Letters: "Ianua: Day Zero plus Three," "Ianua: Day Zero plus Twenty-One"

Asheville Review: "The Lions of Chauvet"

Atlanta Review: "64 Unbekannte Tote: Photograph, Germany, 1970"

Briar Cliff Review: "The Alchemist," "Ianua: 19 September 2016"

Crab Orchard Review: "Ianua: My Father's Rhythm Strip"

Cutthroat: A Journal of the Arts: "Venus Showing Mars Her Doves Making a Nest in His Helmet"

Dogwood: A Journal of Poetry and Prose: "The Return of the Insect Collector, Germany, 2007"

Mid-American Review: "The Shipping Forecast"

Nimrod International Journal: "My Mother's Teeth"

Sow's Ear Poetry Review: "Fossil Hunting at John Lennon Airport, Liverpool," "Still Life with Hand Grenades and Tulips"

Strokestown Poetry, Ireland: "Field Notes: Watching the Crew of Atlantis Renovating the Hubble Telescope"

The Moth: "Disco Jesus and the Wavering Virgins in Berlin, 2011," "Dead Drift"

Three critical pieces of information are needed to carry out dead reckoning: (1) a starting location, (2) a knowledge of the direction you are moving in at all times, and (3) a knowledge of how far you have travelled.

The concept is simple: you deduce your location through a history of your travels from a starting point to your current location.

JOHN EDWARD HUTH, *The Lost Art of Finding Our Way*

Contents

Ianua: 19 September 2016

For my father: 18 July 1924 – 4 September 2014

Submerging below the fields'
thin rind of grass and dirt, following
the inclined walkway into
and through that liminal
territory where hart's-tongue and maidenhair
and even the saturated flannels of mosses,
under pressure from ascending darkness, surrender
and return the limestone to itself,
I have entered the earth without dying.
I have walked into the open

heart of the rock and arrived
at the edge of the original entrance—in the light
of my torch a font of water so utterly untroubled
the mind at first perceives it
as a continuance of air;
but far back in the clearness,
the tight, black gullet of the flooded tunnel.

Midweek. Off-season.
I have the guide to myself. But she's
flicking on spotlights and prattling
on about flowstone and draperies.
Pool spars. Cave pearls. So many
words dropping blandly out of her mouth
without echo, until she ceases
her banter and snaps off the spotlights and I hear,
far off, the massive sweating of stone—evidence
of rain let slowly go—and my eyes
feel strangely opened
beneath the roof of the lightless world.
Later, when I walk out, nothing

at all will be different and everything
will have changed—the clouds
long ago moved over and a blackbird's
cleated call caught still on the air,
although the bird itself will be hidden
within a new neighbourhood

deep in the hedge. But for now, in silence,
in a clot of torchlight, we are following
the meandering path of concrete, we are labouring

deeper, and the heart, believing it will find
what it came for, is one step ahead
of reason and ready
to cross the threshold until, after weaving
through the Cathedral and the Crystal Chamber,
after rounding a sudden blind corner
beyond the pillar of the limestone Madonna—

after coming so far through the hard
skirts of the Earth—we are brought
up short by the strung barrier
of a chain-link fence. Above us, the long

memory of the green world. Around us the deep
unbound pieces of the Earth for a while
holding still. Beyond the net of the fence,

where the bolus of the torch beam
widens and bleeds out, darkness is a door
standing ajar. And from this point on, the way

untravelled, uncharted, unlit.
Every road, every path, every turn I take

leads here. And yet why am I here,
father, if I cannot enter?

Dead Reckoning, Part I: Taking Departure

You sort them like an unmade jigsaw
into piles—skin tone, hair colour, body parts—

having found them beneath a shifting
helm of bird and leaf fret

in the wooded hollow
just beyond the marsh, snagged

like scraps of fabric in the briars.
The first signs of trouble

in the kingdom of childhood.
Evidence everywhere of a bloodless

violence—a private battle, but battle
all the same; everywhere the subtle

deckle-edged surf lines
of torn paper—glossy winks

of skin. Mouths (open), eyes (mostly closed); legs
mostly open to a blister-

wet glisten, but here and there a pair
of knickers around a pair

of ankles like a shackle.
And within each mouth, beyond

the lips' blown defences, behind
an even shield wall of teeth,

the tongue's flexible blade vanishing
down the throat's narrowing welcome.

In secret, at night, like a minor god,
you rebuild each one

from pieces pulled at random
so no woman will look like herself

twice, so each woman, glued firmly
onto card and cut free, is a parquetry

of flesh colour, of size and angles.
Even the one without legs who floats

before you on the blue carpet, waist deep
in dark waters. And each act of creation,

divine or not, gives rise
to some new thing, alive

or not, with a will of its own.
This is when you first understand

that flesh partly clothed appears
more naked; here is where flesh

first throws a shadow
in the shape of a body—shadow

of a life still ahead of you.
For which you will never be ready.

You are, of course, not even
a minor god: you are a girl dreaming

of being small enough to slip
inside the world like Thumbelina and discover

your true disguise in such belonging.
The polished shell of the walnut cradle.

The tulip-petal boat
with its oars of white horsehair.

Meals of dew and honey.
And this is when you first understand you will lose

the keys to the kingdom, which is also small,
which is Eden, surely, because The Garden, remember,

is always a place in time: that square mile,
maybe less, from which not one thing

was lacking; those few years (remember?)
when the mind, housed

like the seed of a berry in the flesh
and oblivious to the flesh,

had not yet invented the body as a problem.

Disco Jesus and the Wavering Virgins in Berlin, 2011

Although a man, I no longer want.
I disown and forget all desires of the flesh.

LATE-NIGHT TELEVANGELIST

How convenient, I say, to the dark. Because this
is what I do when I cannot sleep: sit in darkness
flicking through the god channels, sneering
and answering back, while the neon

tetras beneath their flickering tube light weave
their Möbius strip through the wet fire
of the only world they know; while a man
who makes it dishonest for a woman

to disown her desires—a man
whose body becomes, during sex,
one long wound—sleeps across the hall
in a king-size bed. Every scar is a door

and I have never known scars like his: shrapnel,
bullet, knife blade. The English, I told him
once, as I placed the welter of my lips to his damages
one by one, assume the French verb *blesser*—

to wound—means *to bless*; and he,
without remembering he said it,
said: *the way in and the way out—the doors*
to heaven are always small. This is a man who beguiles

even the dirt up from its knees, whose hands
conjure a body for me out of the body I have; and yet
every bed is a death bed; and yet, the only door
out of the body is death. Outside, a great city

16

and its troubled history under rain.
How is it we can be loved
so well and remain so famished still?
I rejoice, says the preacher, *in the celibate life;*

the thought of one day dying
into heaven. Behind him, deep in an alcove,
washed by slow strobes of alternating colour,
Jesus, life-size and on the cross, turns

from blue to red to yellow
and I am back, suddenly,
at those dreadful Youth Club discos—
all cheap lighting and tinny reverb

and hidden pints of liquor—where I
once let a boy called Martin nudge his hand,
centimetre by centimetre—as if
I would not notice—up under my blouse

until it came to rest, fingers spread, clamped
over my left breast like a fleshy starfish.
I let him because he was tall, a bad boy,
every girl's crush. And because my desire

was beginning to acquire a formal structure.
In this life, proclaims the preacher, as Jesus
turns yellow turns orange turns green, *we are all*
under siege, beset by temptations. I watch

as a single tetra, little morsel of colour, breaks
from the neon spackle of the crowd
and drifts upwards to place the dark foyer
of its tiny mouth

against the roof of its world. And what use,
really, is this life, if it's not one long
sheath of longing. *We are all under siege,*
he says, *afflicted, bedevilled, assailed*

by carnality, so let us pray. Let us pray, he says,
for the wavering virgins. Now I say
it is the poet's duty to wait,
to wait in the dark, to wait in the dark

at the world's mercy
for moments such as this. In the beginning
is the word. And the word
is sex. In the beginning is the kiss

that gives rise to the myth of Eden—that bright
landscape unfettered by history
that we create when placing our open mouth
to the open mouth of another

for the very first time. And yet there is
no garden in which the lion ever will
lie down with the lamb. And like this
the whole body becomes an eye turned

to nothing
but its own pleasure. And every time
we lie down to assuage our loneliness,
we find the flesh already there,

waiting. And all we ever want to do
is undo the violence of this world, and yet
that's how we lie down—with need
and avarice. In the beginning, as I remember it,

is a walled garden, staples of croquet hoops
punched into a lawn. Beyond, in a field,
a horse with a tail so long it brushes the grass.
Late summer. Farm work. Room and board

and pocket change for college. Summer's end,
then; cut fields at dusk and hawks slicing low
over the brittle blonde pipes of stubble.
So many lives already undone

by the round scythes of the combine.
At night from my single bed I listen to the pauses
and the breaks in the bicker of the shower
as the farmer's eldest son turns

and twists beneath it in the small bathroom
along the hall. When I imagine his body—which I do,
and often—it's as a series of broad,
quiet rooms inside the rattle of falling water.

He becomes a man made up of absence.
In the beginning (as I remember it) he puts on
his boots and waxed jacket and walks out
with his dog and a shotgun

into the fields. I do not remember
the gun's report, but if I am not with him
why are there pigeons, all flash
and clatter, breaking for the open; why do I feel,

still, the sudden change
in their purchase on the air—a few seconds
of wild churn and scramble before the spin down
into the stubble. There is the unlit weight

of each skull's chamber, the beak's
loose tweezers, the eyes' eclipse.
With the harvest in, with summer over,
with his parents at church again every Sunday,

it is inevitable, really. And afterwards we lie
like moist kindling under the covers and the world
is just as it was, only more so.
Over the fields, first mists of September

unfurling their aprons the colour of iron.
Rooks like black static. A breeze heckling
silver out of the grass until the lawn
is a carpet of knives. It is my job to cut and split

and ransack the nave of each bird,
which his mother will bake with orange juice
and honey. Six birds in a wheel
on a willow pattern plate, a carousel

of pigeons, their bald, glazed wings
like tiny flippers, and what meat there is
latticed by shot. It is 1978. I am eighteen.
The year Sweden outlaws aerosols,

and Markov, Bulgarian defector, is assassinated
with a poisoned umbrella tip, and Egypt
makes peace with Israel and war begins
in Afghanistan and a man more than twice my age

teaches me that the body
is its own reward. And these days
I sleep right through the minor disruption
of my lover's shower, and when I wake

he's at work—in jeans, perhaps, but shaved—
with his feet on the table and a folder
of case notes before him and his gun, unbreakable
heart, in a holster against his ribs. *The hungers*

of the body, says the preacher, *always*
lead us astray. So let us pray.
Outside, the red crumble of tail lights
down Linienstraße. A great city

and its troubled history under rain.
The whole of Europe under the same rain.
A *waver*, I once read, is a young tree
left uncut during the clearing of timber. Rain,

somewhere, loosening its clothes to play wanton
in the fields; rain drumming its fingers
on the green tiers of the trees. The loneliness
of rain that has come so far

touching only one leaf. And where rain is falling
where there are no leaves, a greater loneliness.
Every word for what we are
leads us back to this. *Human,*

from the Latin *humus,* meaning earth. *Flesh,*
from the Greek, related to *sarx,* meaning earthly; meaning,
of man set adrift from the divine. Every word
for what we are brings us back to the dirt. *So yes,* I say,

let us pray. Let there be buttons
abandoning their buttonholes. Let tongues unbuckle,
let watches, let belts. May small change fallen
from pockets be forgotten, never found.

And shy flags of hair swing loose. Storms
inside strokes of wind. The world is full
of alchemy, so let there be questions
and demands. Small talk, dirty talk, language

in all denominations. Let keys drop and fingers find
every latch and lock and legs peel free
from the sheer, long throats of stockings. Let hearts
be up to their necks in longing.

May jackets and shirts turn inside out;
may the body—in rooms specially rented,
in cars, on tables, in single beds
on Sundays. *Body*, believed to be related to Old Norse

buthker, meaning box; as in, coffin
that goes into the earth. And when the virgins
go down may they go down like heavy crops
go down before the cutter—without choice

and ripe with rains and sugar. Jesus, abandoned
on the cross, alone in his alcove, turns
from green, back to blue, back to red,
while in its tank that single tetra forms perfect

circles on the water simply by drifting
to the surface and kissing what imprisons it.
Why, if desire is so perilous, are we given a god
so obviously human, with an athlete's body, lean

and well-worked; a god whose loincloth is slipping,
pulled down by its own slight weight
over one hip; who has, still, despite all
that's been done to him, such beautiful hands.

A god whose crown is askew,
whose hair needs washing, whose wounds
will become the most terrible of scars.
A god who may well

have desired a woman who made desire pay.
Who may well have been her lover.
Who dies with his arms wide open.

Still Life with Hand Grenades and Tulips

The Somme battlefields, France, 2007

I have family, she says, flailing
her arm in an arc, shunting the vambrace of bangles
on her lean suntanned forearm

towards a dry, metallic music and taking in
the whole of Picardy, *out there. Somewhere.*
She means a man, a great-grandfather,

disappeared ninety years ago now
beneath the rank meniscus of soil,
the churned soup of the fields

closing over him. A man married to a woman
who will spend her best years on a quest
to discover precisely where he fell

before she gives in, quietly, and out in the new
and difficult fields begins sleeping rough
under the thinnest blanket she can find.

Such waste, she says, her lips puckered
by an invisible drawstring of disapproval.
Such waste. And I am not sure

if she is speaking about a man's life
or the sanity of a woman who abandoned
her children, who never remarried, who slept

on the unmarked grave that is this world,
who slept against the skin of this world
that was his grave. Each day I have walked

new paths between fields of sugar beet and barley.
To La Boisselle and The Glory Hole and Tara Hill,
to Thiepval and Hamel and Beaumont Hamel.

To Contalmaison and beyond, through the beeches
and the oaks of Delville Wood and High Wood—
renowned, before the war, for their limes

and hazels, for their hornbeams and chestnuts—
and back, today, through Mametz
and Queen's Redoubt, and on to a small café

in Albert, across from the basilica, where this girl
wearing too many bangles and a low-cut,
tightly-bodiced dress of pale blue cotton

serves me coffee and the chef's daily special
on a patio hemmed with tubs
of tulips—ad rems, she tells me,

and red emperors, grown
every year from bulbs purchased fresh
at a garden centre near Bapaume.

They balance like red flagons
above bluish strap-shaped leaves.
They are, she says, *comme des cœurs.*

Like hearts. The way they close
at dusk, hoarding all night
an emptiness of their own making.

And there are fields here, she tells me,
where cattle won't graze, where they press
against the hedges shifting

from hoof to hoof. Where such fields are
exactly she can't say, and any cattle
I have seen are docile and pacific, tearing

the grass with terrible efficiency,
up to their fetlocks in green.
Once, I stood a whole afternoon and listened

to it happening: grass turning back into bone
and breath and flesh. These fields, I could tell her,
were once windows swinging open so darkness

blew through unsupervised; they were fields
of the narrow escape, of storm. Fields of metal,
banged shut, certain death. Fields that became

floors of water inside a world of rain.
Even though (she admits) she's seen hand grenades
embedded in and flush

with the farmyard cobbles
and followed the shallow contours
of the Newfoundlander's trenches

at Beaumont Hamel, she wants to know
why I'm here when there is nothing
much to see, really, except field after field of wheat

and barley, of beets and flax. It's true,
of course: almost everything that can be
has been salvaged from the edges and fence lines

of these fields—wire and bullets, helmets and pickets,
duckboards, buttons, scattershot of bone.
And although it may be tempting, my guidebook

warns, *to stroll across the worked fields, be advised
such expeditions are unwise and dangerous
and can be fatal. And do not forget*

the thousands still buried here. Meaning: get down
on your knees—even in a tour group of strangers
get down on your knees. And think of the men

who had so much need of and so little time
for god. All about us, mile after mile,
ravaged fields, restored. Open fields, closed. Fields

from which farmers in their reinforced tractors
still reap an iron harvest—a vast
live tonnage of mortars and shells and slim

canisters of White Star, of phosgene
and chlorine—which they leave
in neat rows along the verges of roads

where the foxgloves bloom, slowly,
from the bottom up, each stem unfastening
tier by tier. Here and there a field

rouging its cheeks with poppies. And I
had no idea that such fields under trees
laden with apples could be so beautiful.

Strings of lights blinking on around the square.
The tulips in the dusk begin their slow
closure. And she is so young, and the young,

as they should be, are immune to history. *Really*,
I tell her, pushing back my chair, placing
my payment and a small gratuity, carefully, coin

by coin, down on the table, *I don't know*
why I am here. Even though
what I want to say is: *this, I came here*

for this—to meet a girl who grows tulips
and discover how like such flowers we are, the red
void of our lives an exit

fallen into flame; to inherit the story
of a woman who
at night, for love, lay down in these fields

and endured, for love,
the absence of love.
Because fields that feel so empty still

contain so many. Because death let poetry into my house
and this is my work: to remember whatever it is
that is now no body at all.

The Shipping Forecast

Darkness outside. Inside, the radio's prayer—
Rockall. Malin. Dogger. Finisterre.

CAROL ANN DUFFY

Storms are walking the waters
of Viking and Utsire, and there are gale-force winds
from FitzRoy to Shannon, and for days

a rain so persistent it seems still,
like something solid fixed to the garden.
But everything moves, even the dead. The Earth

is moving them for us. This, then,
is what it comes to: Earth spin, rain and wind.
Remember, she would say, as a form of comfort

when I was a child, *worse things*
happen at sea. Early evening. Dinner over
and table cleared, she would stop

whatever it was she was doing—in her hands
the white disc of a plate,
or a clutch of rinsed utensils, bodies

like the stems of silver grasses. And all
of us would listen, mute and motionless,
for three minutes of common gratitude: Malin,

Hebrides, Bailey, Fair Isle. Dogger.
Fisher. German Bight. It was better than prayer.
Sheeted and safely tucked into the dark's

back pocket, I would dream of great trawlers
moving, inevitably, into fearsome weather.
The chewed edge of a bow wave,

and a handful of following gulls cuffed
back and forth through night's black wall
into the reach of the running lights. There were men,

too—northern pirates from Grimsby or Hull—
going out like boys, full-lunged
among their own kind, with tales of winter stars

that snapped like dogs. And I was young,
of course; of course I was a child, but this
is how it came to pass that I can love

only men who are willing to inhabit
the darkness I have invented for them.
October. Darkness running aground by five o'clock.

Now and then, the distant, unfaltering grind
of a westbound jet, heading out
across the Atlantic. Even now, when I

am a child no longer and her skin
has been debrided by drugs
and by chemicals, my mother looks at me

and says, *worse things, remember,*
happen at sea. Bedridden, barely speaking,
sending her words out like castaways

on short rafts of breath. She is a few days out
from death. We know it. Without knowing
we know it. There is nothing

worse than this. And each morning I run the fine
dark bristles of an expensive brush
with a tortoiseshell handle through her hair.

I am reading, keeping vigil beside her,
surprising myself with my appetite
for murder because in every story

there is death dressed up in abstractions—passion,
madness, grief, revenge; here is death
at the hands of others—by bullet, by Semtex, by Sarin,

by machete. No sound but the rasp
and catch of her breathing and a faint
agitation as with the heel

of her left palm anchored firmly she lifts
each finger in turn into a flutter, then a ripple,
then an undulation against the covers. For the first time

in fifty years, that hand bereft
of its ring. Which had slipped off, somewhere,
as illness belittled every part of her. A ring

is open-mouthed, like rain.
I remember my father emptying the hoover
onto newspapers neatly spread

over the beige linoleum, sifting dust
from one page to another. I remember him
in his privet-green wellingtons

down on his knees before every flowerbed.
If my ring were lost in the garden, she'd said,
perhaps ravens have come down

off the hills, as they do, for bright things.
I could live with a loss like that.
We are still hoping.

And because I think it will calm her,
I brush her hair, relishing its slight resistance,
the faint clicks of static;

and I place my hand, like a little roof,
over her hand, but her fingers
keep moving and there is nothing fleeting

or feathery about it—it is nothing at all
like the fremitus of startled birds or the forays
of wind through long grasses. Her touch

is determined, insistent, like the muscled heave
of water, like a wave, which is, after all,
merely energy passing through matter.

And you simply cannot argue
with the muscularity of water. Even my father—
who has been holding out

before the rising battlements
of her coma, offering up on a teaspoon
pale slumps of apple sauce and honey—

cannot quiet her, until from a box
on the dresser he takes a ring—too large,
too heavy, a single pearl

in a noose of sapphires—and threads
her finger through it. And some fretting animal
lowers its head at last to rest. Everything moves.

Even the dead. The Earth is moving them for us.
And there are storms walking the waters
of Viking and Utsire, and gale-force winds

from FitzRoy to Shannon, and this
is what it comes to: Earth spin, wind and rain.
I shall remember how I was grateful

for every hour death kept us waiting.
I shall remember how when her hand fell still
I missed its movement. Pale flag

of an overrun country. How even my father's hands
could not calm her. How I did not brush
the fine waves of my mother's hair enough.

Ianua: Day Zero plus Three

I take an inch of hair, cut
from that subtle overlooked curve
of bone behind the ear. The sound,

inside the room's quiet, like the tearing
of grass—expansive and final. I take
only what I can hold, like the soft white hair

of a paintbrush, in the plump
ferrule I make of a forefinger
and thumb. Because my father's hair

is white, but not at all like snow and nothing
at all like ivory—the poverty of clichés,
the dangers of living

a life through language. So instead
let's say my father's hair is like the stems
of marram wet from a sudden squall

of rain and whipped white by the wind
in the light. Etchings on glass.
And I think of Rubens choosing to render

the flash of Delilah's doubt and regret;
how, in that endless moment right
before the cut, as the light from the lantern

catches and holds on the fulcrum
of the scissors' pivot, we see in her face
an echo of knowledge surfacing: it's too

late, it's too late, now, it's sunlight caught
in play on the blade of a scythe. And Samson,
of course, is sleeping, adorning

the lap of his lover, unprotected
by the shield of his own self-awareness; his beauty
more astonishing because

he is sleeping. And as his companions
moil at the threshold of the chamber,
the Philistine positions his scissors. But I

have no doubt.
And my father is not sleeping.
He is visible from the waist up,

lying in the silk-frilled mollusc
of his coffin. Against the inside
of my body, like a new lining, the pressed ache

of grievance: that a stranger
washed my father's hair; that a stranger washed
my father's body. I want to unbutton

his shirt; I want to unbutton
it all the way and find, in that shallow
hollow where neck meets clavicle, the incision

through which the stranger who washed
my father's hair hooked a vein, then lifted
it free, then bled

this body. In the apex of the belly's apse
I'll find that chirp of a wound
from the surgeon's needle. The button

of the trocar. Damage
from the childhood injury that almost
killed him; long weld of the scar from the bullet

that should have—my father
never could say why, on the banks
of the Rhine, in the dawn of a late-March

morning, he unfolded himself from the dirt
of his slit trench and became a man
against the skyline. And in his heart there is a wound

like a mouth, now, where no
mouth should be. Lipless. A mouth
without language. And to see that, to find

what killed him, I'd be tender—no more
violence, no more breakage; I'd open
him up as if opening

up a way through water, my palms moving
through each glide and catch
until I reach the heart's wrung meat

beneath its thin-slatted baldachin
of bone. I look for the last time
at the body of my father. I put away

my small scissors. I walk from the room
with my white brushstroke of hair.

Venus Showing Mars Her Doves
Making a Nest in His Helmet

After a painting of the same name by Joseph-Marie Vien
in The Hermitage, St. Petersburg, Russia

A rosary of crows in white air. Along the Neva
a breeze bending at the waist like a woman.
And a pigeon muttering, somewhere, smooth
and fluent, almost beyond hearing.

So. What would you like to do, you ask,
for the rest of the day? Alarming,
the hard beauty of your body; the daily
injuries of which you know nothing
simply fixing themselves. *I don't care,*

I say. From the guidebook you are reading
we learn that in '41 the galleries
we'd strolled all morning had been emptied;
The Bronze Horseman in Senate Square
sandbagged and camouflaged;

how those left trapped in a city under siege
had eaten their dead, and heavy loaves
of sawdust and linseed. And all I really want
is to stay right here, at this table on the terrace
of The Pushka, pouring tea and passing, without being asked,

white rolls and curls of sweet unsalted butter
as the birds around us go public
with their private desires, and the breeze runs its feints
and pale havoc along the skin of the river; while our terrors
doze in the grass of the body's fields, which are unfenced.
With your hands unsheathed of harm. *History,*

I say, *writes nothing but elegies.* Even though
I want to believe a man can be distracted
by pleasure; that desire's aftermath
can leave him grateful, and generous; that life
can trick him into working
towards its own purpose. Even though,

just that morning, we'd entered the quiet
chain of galleries and encountered in Room 52
between the paintings of David and Le Brun,
Mars and Venus, virtually naked, standing
in an amphitheatre of pillars and thick foliage
where a pre-storm light lays its unguent
down on the dark tongues of the trees.
And Mars, of course, is tanned

and muscled. Of course he is beautiful,
and terrible, his armour tossed down in the dust
so we are forced to acknowledge the fleshy
spill of his skirt leather and those swirled, raised nipples
in the bronze of his cuirass and the red slow pour
of his plume across the dirt. And Venus, the pale yoke

of an arm placed around his shoulder, offers
the blush challenge of her doves on their little froth
of twigs and sticks. She's known from the start
that he'll shrug off the shackle of her arm

and reach for his armour; she's ready
for the fluster and metallic tocsin of her doves'
small claws against the curve of his helmet
as they lift off in a cough of feathers. And you

are reading about the mortal duty of the artist to protect
that which is immortal, but, really, there is so
little time for god in a lifetime of searching, and I think
I hear the words *beauty* and *eternal* but am distracted

by your profile, by the fragile rafter of your neck exposed
between shirt collar and hairline as you bend

over the glossy pages of the guidebook, its spine flaring wide
with a series of delicate snaps.

Dead Reckoning, Part II:
Marking One's Position

To begin, to enter the gateway
of each blank page torn from the sketchbook,

you pry the lid from the oblong box. Inside,
in a white tray, the mosaic of your palette:

twenty-four small tiles of watercolour.
Your obvious preferences—mint green

and cerulean, red ochre and black—
brush-worn down into hollows. You unroll

the long bandolier
of felt-tip pens—a glittering fifty-piece set

of fearsome ammunition; you arrange your pencils,
your chalks and wax crayons; you take

up your brushes and bow, in turn, over each
unmarked expanse of paper, creating for each

new woman a portion of paradise
that will remain hers

alone. For one, the gated backroad cemetery.
Spittle of white stones. Crow's black glove.

And there, where sunlight is forcing the green
hands of the grass, you fasten her

down. For another, seethe of pasture
where horses graze, bees and common blues

above trefoil and restharrow. And the sky's
blue lapping joined to the derma of the Earth

by a long, thin frenulum of haze.
And your favourite, the one already

waist deep in dark waters, you suspend
between silt and air, between nightmare

and rapture: over her, neon stitchings
of blue emperors and common hawkers; water

chivvied by wind. She is part of a world,
now, whose treasure is fitfully given; a world

without light; a world with no depth
or distance until through that dimness,

like a small black dragon, wafts
a newt's truly solid darkness. Around her,

the velvet batons of cattails. Over her,
on the surface, lilies with the bolts

of their unshot blossoms. And the dragonflies' hunger,
which has, like their future memory

of wings, been here all along.
It makes no difference that you

have given each of these women a new body—
look, even the blue emperor abandons

the hard armour of its carnivorous life
to become an equally ravenous

skewer of sex. It makes no difference
how you position them. They all still lie

there. Nursing death. Waiting to be seen.

Fossil Hunting at John Lennon Airport, Liverpool

On 25 July 2005, John Lennon Airport unveiled its new terminal building. Although technically JLA is a state-of-the art building, inside it is constructed of limestone slabs that contain fossils of creatures that lived up to 250 million years ago. The limestone is from a quarry near the small town of Solnhofen in Germany. Today, Solnhofen's owners, with the cooperation of the German government, allow visitors to hunt for fossils and take them home without filing reports or paying duty. The slabs of the airport contain millions of fossils.

> JOE CROSSLEY
> "A Guide to the Geology of John Lennon Airport"

LIVERPOOL

There is something reminiscent of trust,
of a living animal curled in on itself
and tightly sleeping; something disturbing
in the way it is sliced so cleanly
open, exposing the dark
undulations of the septa, like curtains,
between each chamber. On Level 2
the statue of Lennon is striding over
the largest ammonite in the airport,
but I like this one, here, on Level 1,
on the floor of the ladies' toilets,
third stall from the left; and I am thinking
about harm and vulnerability when the door
to the stall next to mine bursts open,
then closes. I hear the chrome latch rattle
into its bracket, and then, suddenly,
she is talking and weeping at the same time—
something about a brother in Geneva
who fell from a scaffold and is locked
in a coma, and I realise she's on her mobile,
and her parents, I discover, are on holiday

in Seville. And she can't reach them.
There's the little storm of someone
brushing their teeth, taps
blurting on, then off, and an insect
chorus of handbags and cases
zippering open. She could have left sooner,
she says, but couldn't find her passport,
and now, she says, she is certain
she won't reach him in time. Between us,
where the thin partition doesn't meet the floor,
the small, dark, and perfect torpedo
of a fossil I cannot name. She's on the next flight out,
she says, which leaves in two hours and *oh god*,
she says, *we are all so alone and I feel so afraid*
and I just wish I could hold you. I watch
the fretting shadow of her hand as she talks.
Three hours later, halfway to Berlin, I'm weeping
into my complimentary in-flight beverage,
with nothing but static on the audio,
which I listen to anyway because static,
I read, is remnants and tatters
of the Big Bang, and because I am thinking
about that woman on her way to Geneva—
the place where antimatter was trapped at last
for a tenth of a second, and *half the universe*,
one scientist said, *has gone missing,*
so some kind of rethink is on the agenda.
What hope is there when even the gods
we invent can be known only by their absence.
In Schönefeld my passport vanishes
beneath the bulletproof window
and is handed back. And then the frosted
doors whisper smoothly apart like curtains
and there he is—the man I desire
beyond all reason, lounging in a black

upholstered chair. *How was your flight,*
he says, and I nearly fold down onto my knees
before him and say, there's a woman,
right now, in Geneva, beside the bed
of her comatose brother and I spent two hours
looking at fossils and have been undone
by the evidence of life's lost argument
with time and, oh god, we are all so alone
and I feel so afraid, and the whole way here
I was tuned in to the residual radiation
of the universe, weeping into my tomato juice
and pretzels. But I wait for him to stand

and then I take him into my arms and I hold him.
I simply hold him. *It was fine*, I say. *Just fine.*

INTERMISSION IN BERLIN

The sweatshop of summer and the mute ache
of noon along the limb of the river

and the table's blue umbrella has us
in the diffused climate of its colour. On the streets

women bare their skin and, this being Europe,
wear their nipples like jewellery. And I am tired

of how lust between people passing on the pavements
rises up with no history attached, even though

there have been men with whom I was naked
only once. My lover is heedless of everything

but his Linzertorte and latte, and I begin to talk
about the woman in Geneva, about her brother,

and her parents—who, even then perhaps, were oblivious
still and happy somewhere in Spain—and the fossils

with the secret rooms of their bodies
fixed open. After two hours, I say, of scrutiny,

what I liked best were all the traces, all
those clues of passage—the tail tracks and footprints,

the burrows and castings—because this, I say,
is what art is, after all: not the physical

evidence of the body, but the record
of its forays into daily living. *Every metaphor,*

he says, leaning back in his chair, *is a lie.* Yes,
I think, every metaphor is a lie, and that

is its triumph because it has us believing
in what we cannot see, because the world is always

other than what it is. And I think about how
when I undress him, freeing small buttons, stripping

back layers, it's because I want to believe
there is somewhere further to go. *There is,* I say,

leaning over to pinch the last of his torte,
somewhere I want you to take me. Behind him

the willows along the river trail their long green knives.

SOLNHOFEN

We take a room at the Gasthof Sonne
with its window boxes of petunias
and sweet alyssum. We have a view
of the garden, its lawn striped and crisp

from the shuttle of a recent mowing. Limestone,
we read over breakfast, is not quarried,
but won, and won by hand, and it's been won
here, by hand, since the Romans first favoured it

for their floors and walls. At the public quarry
we pay our fee; we unpack our brushes
and gloves, our chisels and mallets, and begin
on the winnings the Master of the Quarry

rejected after tapping every single plate
with his hammer, listening for the pure,
high note of unflawed stone. All morning
on our knees we work, talking about the Romans

who dug here, who measured and displayed
their fossils, who ploughed up bones and massive teeth
from the fields and from them created
their myths of giants and heroes. *For whither,*

asked Lucretius, *shall we make appeal? for what*
more certain than our senses can there be
whereby to mark asunder error and truth?
But that empire is gone. I think of my parents

inside the long fists of their coffins; of that man
in Geneva, who may have already abandoned
the antechamber of his coma and become,
even for his sister, nothing but history;

I think of the fossils, the coils
of their diminishing rooms, of how
I'd stood, head bowed, while those around me
queued at check-in with their fussy carry-ons,

flashing passports, unpocketing keys
and coins and stepping out of their shoes
and folding their coats and jackets,
and then waiting, while those trays

holding all their belongings moved away
like little grey boats, until, waved forwards,
they passed, one by one, through
to the other side. And even though the body's

nakedness is not a metaphor, I want to place
my hand on the nape of my lover's neck;
I want to beguile him back to that hotel bed
with its sheets of Egyptian cotton,

the wrapped sweet on each fat pillow.
But I can tell he is a man who has, for now,
escaped even the necessity of his body—
that every lust and discomfort, every ache

and hunger, has fallen away and, yes,
every metaphor is a lie, but the point
is to keep your eyes on those rafts of stone and admit
that the dead stay dead forever, and recognise

between two oblivions this brief, dream-slick
threshold each one of us calls our life. And so,
I simply watch him as he labours, as he adds
to the scree pile of treasures beside him, shirtless,

head bowed, on his knees, his torso flowered with dust.

Dead Drift

Water shelving off into darkness and the mind,
which accepts the river's depth, is perplexed
by the eyes' denial. Flat as shadow

on grass you lie, watching the mouth
of the net held close to the bank, waiting
for a wide-open, astonished eye, for a wedge
of head to cohere out of silt and present
itself, as all beings born into time
do, with defiance and out of matter
both moving and held
motionless in suspension. Then the quick

veer, the glint-thrill, the solid, flexed silm
of a body at the surface as it turns. After that,
the backwash, a sluggish roil, the vane of a tail

receding. *Where was I*, you think, *before I
was suddenly here—cleaved cell, a gyre*

of code unlocked? In the net's uneasy
alchemy each brown trout
rests, finning in place, nose to the current,
until your father, who caught each fish and slipped
each hook and holds the net, submerges

its rim and decants each life back
into the flow of the river—not a fish, not a trout, no
nameable shape—just a finned smear, a flare
of copper. Then nothing but your own reflection
restored to the water's surface as the water
restores its mirror. Early evening, a sudden

coolness filming the skin and, as if
some marvelous army has placed its shield wall
to rest, canted sunlight falling

in blazons on the water. Here, for a while, before
humping north to face the tribes
of Caledonia, a small and weary detachment
from the Ninth Legion of Rome did
place their shields and their weapons down,
right here, on the banks of the Wharfe,
and named their settlement Calcaria, meaning
lime. The pale blocks of empire quarried, right here,
by slaves, on territory stolen from the Celtic tribes,
on the great north road to Eboracum.
But before all this—before the Brigantes

and Romans and Vikings and French, before flints
and axes and spear-blades; before the age
of long barrows and dolmens; before the first
brattle of war and occupation and every
advance and obliteration of history, there was stone
and the stone's own story of molluscs and forams
and corals. Evidence of oceans, of time's
crushing indifference. Out in that river,

in chest-high waders, your father is loading
his rod for the cast; the loop of the line unfurls
and the fly—a Pale Evening Dun—settles
on a seam where two currents meet and

dead drifts to where eddies mark a trout
sipping mayfly from the surface. Not once
have you asked your father why, when he crimps
the barbs flat against the shank of every hook and files
them smooth and then releases
every fish he fights and fatigues and plays

into the net, he even fishes at all. Perhaps
it has something to do with how the fly
presents itself perfectly on the water; or the line,

a filament of sky come loose, unfurling. No, not the fly,
or the line, but his arm casting. No, not that: not

the casting, but the arm lifting, suddenly,
to set the hook. No not even the arm,
but the whole body reacting. A river
is a closed door that opens everywhere
and always and only into itself and in the long,
continuous lick of its current is a man
standing motionless, braced

for the strike. And before there was pigment,
before the first flute, before fire; and until all the hands
silhouetted in ochre, until the aurochs and ibex
and spotted horses walked out of the mind as the mind
unhooked itself from darkness,
there was this: the whole body reacting—animal,
instinctive. And after? Not the reaction,

but the seconds it took—not many, but one; no,
not even one, not the seconds at all,
but that fraction of unmeasurable time in which

whatever was about to be done
remained undone.

The Alchemist

To imagine a language is to imagine a form of life.

LUDWIG WITTGENSTEIN

Downstream in the neon blades
of their bodies the dragonflies patrol the borders
of their invisible kingdoms.

Loud and careless, the boys
come surging through the slough grass,
crushing the jewel weeds' freckled pitchers
and the purple spears of loosestrife;

and the sunlight unfastening
through the shallow water opens
into weals of bronze—mouths
in which the smallest fish become visible.

And yet, in less than a minute, those boys
with their unnamed desires churn
the clarity to milt. The boys

of my childhood always came
in a dark rush, tongues of cardboard
gargling between the spokes of each front wheel,
to fling toads and frogs (the perfect
dark-green fruits of their bodies) under cars, down
in the dip where the stream slipped into
a culvert beneath the road.

Bright harm of bicycles
sown among the rushes and cord grass;

sticklebacks on the stream bank madly
slapping the dirt as if the dirt
might open its door
and let them in.

And there were catapults and there were
stones, and there were fledglings
scrambling for leverage in the air's
bright chute, a second or two
of gliding none could sustain.
And survivors, who kept the stretched
funnels of their beaks wide open, were fed
pebbles and twigs and string.

I remember beaks closing
and opening. I remember a rending
that had no sound. I remember

the mouth's wet threshold. Bodies in prayer.
Bodies on fire. Televisions with the sound
turned down because silence made sense
of the women weeping.
A solitary ox still towing its plough
through a rice field, fetlock deep in isinglass.
And soldiers everywhere in staggered file,
festooned with bandoliers
of ammunition. And that girl

who witnessed everything, what defence can I claim,
now, for her? The boys were always slipping
behind the tree line's scrim, a jigsaw
of bright shirts and leaves and the hard

sheen of hair; and she is always
there, on the frontier, holding her stance,
holding my gaze, holding me accountable
for the future, of which she is already certain.

This, then, is where we meet, that girl

and I. She knows I have no gods.
She knows when I write that my whole body
becomes a mouth; that I

could disarm those boys of every single
cruelty they go on to commit and so
transform them, in memory, to mere glints
of dread—glass shard, knife blade,
the flensed stick. And the nail, point upward,
in the grass of the garden. Where she

is waiting. With no catapult,
no rock, no rope. No
visible weapon of any kind.

Isis on the Mississippi

For the victims and survivors of the Minneapolis I-35W bridge collapse, 7 August 2007

It's part of family history: the way I stood for hours
before a single painting
in the Egyptian Museum on Boderstraße. Before me,

under glass, Isis in the guise of a falcon parsing
the long tongue of the Nile searching

for the broken, scattered body
of Osiris. Here, the river drags
its dark garments. All day, herons shrug upwards

out of the shallows. Sometimes, small boats pass
and, sometimes, rain falls harmlessly out of silence

back into silence. I know some of you must sleep
and make love with the names of the dead
in your mouths; that you are living

and lost within your own bodies. I know
that everyone's joy must now seem easier

than your own. I cannot tell you how long it took
for Isis to find and gather what was lost; only
that the artist rendered her following her need

into every eddy and side channel, into the bird-filled glister
of papyrus and reed, into the thick smoulder of every

single marsh. A long time. I say *falcon or heron?*
I say even the river must be taken piece by piece
before it can be held in a single hand. I say *the lost one,*

rescued. I say what you remember may well be
the only afterlife there is. So I say *cleave*

together, and I say *gather in;* and I say refuse
to let your words remain broken in your grief.

Field Notes: Watching the Crew of Atlantis Renovating the Hubble Telescope

What comforts me most is imagining the calm,
regular draw and blow of their breathing;
that they are floating, for a while,

    in exile and surviving
    because after weeks of drifting tethered
    to a machine that pulled in
    the room's ambient air, compressed it and vented
    off its nitrogen with such a quiet
    and relentless suck and surge, my mother
    had crossed into the homeland
    no one is equipped to travel through. Tethered

securely, and laden with tools
and equipment, the astronauts bury their arms,
elbow-deep, into the silver torso
of the telescope. Beneath them, across the Earth, night's
precise curve approaching and nothing
around them but the constant
wash of their own breathing. What I remember most

    about my mother's last breath was the way her eyes
    opened slightly—slim buttonholes
    in the body's fabric—and my father rising
    out of his chair to lean over
    the bed's chrome railing, to get as close
    to her as he could, to rest his forehead against hers
    and whisper *hello, Eileen*; and I found myself

    thinking about that white and half-wild
    pony in the pasture next door;
    the way, each morning, behind a single strand
    of fence wire, it waited—a solid, pale patience—
    for my father to trail through the damp
    nap of the lawn with his small offering;

the way it would lower its head, then,
to press against him, with such restraint,
the long, heavy treasure of its skull.
The thick plate of the forehead. Each nostril's
soft cuff. But it was over

already and that machine went on breathing
without her until I rocked its small red switch
into silence. There was the fixed curve
of my father's spine. There was the still weight
of his head against hers. Our first night on Earth
without her. Wind in the hawthorn and the great
carnival wheel of stars. The astronauts

are repairing the gyros; they are fitting
the spectrograph and the wide-field cameras
that will allow us to gaze right onto
the cosmic frontier. And the undertaker unzipped the dark

bloom of his body bag. Later, the froth
of the first birds, and the lights of the fleet roped
three deep along the quay fraying
in a dawn that arrived like wood smoke and,
for a while, my father and I not knowing how
to be with each other. With their gentle

and deliberate gestures the two astronauts
appear almost tender, like lovers.
The visors of their helmets are golden
blisters of reflected light. It is impossible to gauge
the ferocity of thought inside them.

The Lions of Chauvet

*Above all, some of them, a mere handful in any generation, perhaps,
loved—they loved the animals about them, the song of the wind...
On the surfaces of cave walls the three dimensions of the outside world
took animal shape and form. Here—not with the ax, not with the bow—
man fumbled at the door of his true kingdom.*

LOREN EISELEY

The lioness moves like thought, slick
and continuous, into a world imagined
ahead of itself. This great cat
has been lost, even to herself,
for the longest time. Who knows
how an animal grieves. The children arrive
in a rush—driven smoke
or water—and fuse in a sudden crush
against the long barrier
of laminated glass.

> What are we to make of the fact
> that the animals painted with brushes
> of horsehair, with feathers and fingers,
> in the cave of Chauvet are not, primarily,
> animals of the hunt, but predators rendered
> in umbers and ochres, in pigments
> bound with fat and urine and blood, in the blacks
> of scots pine charcoal and burnt bone.

There is tenderness
and something faintly domestic
inside a lion's mouth; in the way
a tongue, even though it rasps skin
from flesh, scours flesh from bone, drapes over
the china-white hooks of incisors
like a length of pink linen.
The lioness places the discs

of her great paws down
in huffs of dust. The scimitars of her claws
she keeps well hidden. And the children
have their hands spread flat against the glass;
they seem so vulnerable—this fidgety
line of little mammals
with their backs to the world.

    In Chauvet, where they cannot be reached
    without effort, without torches, without the fire
    we bring with us, two lions,
    in profile, are walking side by side.
    The line of the male's back—from the muzzle
    through the shoulder and haunch to that bulb
    of fur at the tip of his tail—is one
    continuous gesture. The contour
    of the lioness nests so beautifully inside him.

After the children have gone, all bounce
and jostle, the lioness in her habitat moves
behind a dense stippling of handprints, an exotic
frieze of greasy, pale leaves.

    What are we to make of the fact
    that the entrance chamber of Chauvet
    contains a whole rock panel of hands, a panic
    of palms—the dark extremis of minds
    aware of themselves; that because
    of a kink in a little finger, there is one
    individual we can follow back
    into the cave, print by print, chamber by chamber.

    But to enter—to enter the earth and feel
    the caul of the polished world slip
    from you—you must be invited, you must be
    in the company of the chosen, of one

whose palm, placed down
upon and read by a sensitised plate, breaks
the seal and opens the way. Do not doubt

that there are those who are willing
to sever the hand from the body, willing
to have their last act of freedom
be imprisonment, here, in the calm-black kernel
beneath the green life
of the busy hill, in the company of animals,
of the story's first syllables, the negative
presence of someone whose hand
is held, still, in a flocked aura of ochre
sprayed straight from the mouth.
And the chill
of thirty-three thousand years
between the present
and the drawn line. The first world.

 Which did not exist
  until it came up against the mind and was troubled

into form. Because this
is the beginning. This is the hand
waiting upon and holding within itself
all possible futures. I say the hand
was our very first symbol
for that need felt inside the body

for something beyond the body. I say hands
were our very first language—just watch
the way they flounder to become
an extension of thought when we are speaking.

Later, while shelves are restocked
and money is counted, after the guards' final sweep
and checks, after the gates are locked, the lioness
will be coaxed with a shank of mutton or horse meat
into her windowless pen while her keepers enter
the meagre arena of her habitat, her small agon
of concrete and heated rocks, to wipe down

perches and ledges, to rake
and spot clean the dirt.
And someone with a trolley of cleaners
and cloths and a long–handled mop
will make their way steadily
down the long barrier of glass, spraying
and swiping it clean
of every handprint, every blemish.

    The lions in Chauvet, all force and heft,
    all muscle and breath, walked
    a very long time in darkness, side by side,
    towards the moment of their discovery.

    In that gap between the black
    contour of the lion's back and the back
    of the lioness is a single sinuous line
    of ochre. There are theories: that this was a line

    placed down as a guide
    to positioning; that this is proof of an artist's delight
    in the frisson of colour. What are

    theories if not a means of testing
    our belief about the world. And if belief,
    like the body, is an animal, then flesh
    is the measure of all things. I say

this line is evidence of love
in its purest form: the heart teaching the hand
what to put in, what to leave out; I say

someone witnessed, and understood, the third
animal these lions dragged into the world

in the wake of their affection. Because these lions
have been abstracted into life by the prayer
of attention. Their bodies are touching as they walk.

Aries

Under the wind's blunt touch the long
body of the hedge twitching
like an animal. All day you work, trying

to escape the life you've been given. Beyond

the hedge a solitary ram
blinkered by his horns. Each time
rain moves through he shakes off
like a dog, his packed fleece rocking.

You keep working, and looking up,
even after the dark has run its rasp in
over the fields.

All day you kept looking

up from the page to see where he was
as he lived his one life in the meadow.

Anti-Pastoral for Myself as a Child

Crying to the gods of the downs till their brains were turning
And the gods came.

JOHN MASEFIELD

I

A scythe forgotten, dropped
like a weapon in the half-down grasses.

Sudden breeze-shear and then
the blether of rain—persistent
rain, and the cutters have abandoned
their mowing; will leave the hay ungathered.

II

The dirt begins its list of stillness:
cleaved mouse, split vole; the nest of a skylark, riven.

III

Everything, now, could reach for redress; gods
might come: one vagrant
god inside the rain and green
might sing its way out through the door
of each cut blade of grass.

IV

But this undoing never should
become a bruise of light; the hurt

inside the kiss should never
grow a song.

V

There must be no
atonement for such ruination,
child. Cleaved mouse. Split vole. The nest
of a skylark, riven.

64 Unbekannte Tote: Photograph, Germany, 1970

On sloped ground next to the playing field
she has built, for herself alone, an almost human
figure—faceless, sexless, with the smooth,
glazed coat snow acquires when over-handled
and compressed. To her left, beyond the pale
slim border of the picture, is the house
she lives in; the house from which she rides
her white three-speed bicycle—out
through the front gate, over the cricket pitch, down
past the pig farm and into the ruins
of Bergen-Belsen; a house that contained
at the end of the war eight hundred
sixty-nine Gypsies, Jews, and "others"—overflow
from the camp, as Stalin advanced and Hitler panicked
and prisoners were shuffled west. To her right,
just out of view, is the unkempt cemetery
in which, three decades from now,
the bones of sixty-four bodies will be reburied
between a cedar and the green gumline of a hedge
in a grave the size of a double bed
after being uncovered by German workers
breaking ground for a new gymnasium

right where she is standing, right under her feet.
She is ten, adept at dropping her net
over resting insects: peacock, stonefly, sulphur yellow;
mantis, cockchafer, devil's coach-horse.
In her small room, on plastic fold-out tables,
a precise arrangement of bodies and every
specimen labelled with region, with country,
with nearest town; with host plant and date
of collection. Her curiosity, you know now,
is fuelled by love. For now,
her daily regrets are so small the rain
devours them overnight and she can sleep

without dreaming in that house. For now
she is simply a child squinting against snow
and sunlight, and beneath that snow
and the soles of her black boots, bones
in their mass grave. And by the time she returns

here she will be almost fifty and those dead,
without her knowing, will have followed
her through every poem and into every
bed, and the sun will be holding hands
with the shadows as she stands on the curb
of their new grave. But for now she is a child

so in love with the world: ground beetle,
copper, clouded apollo; wood wasp, fritillary,
alpine argus. And she does not know it yet,
of course, but this girl will one day become
your most valuable lost possession: this girl
bludgeoned by sunlight, with a heart

like a beetle under bark, in a world
where death has not yet connected the dream
and the dwelling place.

Ianua: My Father's Rhythm Strip

To you, line unforeseen or always known.

RAFAEL ALBERTI

I

To Lórien Knoll from Rockall Bank
and on, then, to Isengard Ridge, to Thulean Rise,
to Orphan Basin and the Flemish Cap:

the route you'd plot, when asked,
to Newfoundland from the coast of Éire
on profile maps of the Atlantic

floor, those maps you'd loved—all ridges
and valleys and abyssal plains.
Running all through my life, this chain

of names. The longest range
of mountains in the world, you'd said, right
there beneath the ocean's indifferent preening;

guyots and seamounts, and trenches
five miles deep. A darkness, you'd said, that is
not simply an absence

of light, but an element even older perhaps
than light—the black vice of matter
before time. But the beauty of those names:

who could fail to fall in love with darkness
when it held such sounds.

II

Imagine a man
strolling through the smell of smoke
and horses and the loose gutted bodies

of the morning catch to board a ship
that departs with the ebb under a chorus
of sails; a man who climbs the ladder to ride

the yaw in the crow's nest. How long,
on observing some small change
coming over the curve of the Earth—land

scrolling towards him, needle of a mast, hand
of a sail—would that man
have remained silent, unwilling to relinquish

his uniqueness; secluded and alone
in his discovery? Even after
your death something kept coming into being

along the paper. But it was only a machine
revealing that your blood had fallen finally
quiet inside the walls of its prison.

It was after all, then, a single moment—
your death: not a place
of continual arrival; not

the apparent juncture of sky and water.

III

Think of that flare deep in the gut—love's
visceral engine—when our lines match up
with the shapes of our longing.

Because love exists
before logic or language. Why else
would the painters of the caves, aware perhaps

of the mind's growing sharpness, hide
their animals in darkness.
Think of the lines we have drawn between stars

so the emptiness they outline
might be, for a while, diminished; so the darkness
we inherit is familiar. And what of the daughter

of Butades the potter, in love
with a boy from Corinth, a boy who would vanish
into the extremis of war; how she traced

on the wall his shadow's outline as he
lay sleeping on the slender catafalque
of her bed. There are several versions:

that his shadow was cast
by a candle, by a lantern, by moonlight
reflecting off the Gulf of Corinth. It makes no difference.

IV

Every boundary, every outline, even
when given its name, contains
its emptiness to the end: auroch, lion,

bison, deer; The Net, The Archer,
the beloved's body. As a child
I drew nothing but horses—in outline,

in profile; on test papers, in notebooks,
in a novel's margins: chin groove, throat latch
and the mass of the gaskin, the slope

of a hoof's front wall for which there is
still no name. I drew them life-size
in dirt, in mud; I wanted an open solitude, another life,

a body I could step into and inhabit.
Which I did.   I have eighteen feet of paper—
a narrow strip. I choose a circle. I join

each end with tape. A corral
large enough to enter. Which I will. I could even
lie down and sleep and safely

dream inside the final moments
of your life. And I will. Yet what
are dreams if not memory at work

inside the body, which is flesh
and knows only the moment. When I wake
there will be nothing but the mouth

of each empty doorway; each empty
doorway's line of threshold. And the flimsy
paper circle of your absence.

And what is emptiness in the end
if not a form of waiting: think of all
the words there must be, even now,

waiting for a language; of a lake's mirror
ready for birds and cloud; of how
we empty ourselves of ourselves

in the hope that our dead
will enter and discover evidence
of their own existence. Of the solid quiet

of a field in summer
emptied of cattle, who have followed each other
into the cool stillness of the milk barn: the lure

of a pasture, briefly abandoned, light
still burning in its one green window; the temptation

of a gate standing fully open.

Dead Reckoning, Part III: Set and Drift

So. Untroubled. Unburdened by everything
the body was destined to become, you'd waded

home through the annealed light of evening
with your glass jar of pond weeds and water.

Bees plundering the hollow horns
of white clover. The workers of a hive,

it is true, wear out their wings
in a sweet, short life; and honey—the syrup

of flowers, the bees' modest embalming—
has been found, it is true, incorrupt

in the tombs of the Pharaohs, even though
it had been left there to be eaten;

even though it had been left there to sweeten
the darkness. Spring in Europe.

Oaks and beeches flouting their leaves
like newly polished nails.

Within your jar, inside the liquid's gimbal,
palm-hauls of spawn—common

grass frog you were certain—swivelled
suspended always on the level, parallel,

always, to the earth. In the flask
of your small body a fluent, blunt

hunger for the world; and those women
in pieces in the briars, desirable. And so

you'd simply gathered them
to you, as you did the feathers

of the yellowhammer on its woven
nest of spider silk and grasses; as you did

the fruiting bodies of the pine mushroom—night's
outriders, urgings of soil made solid—

with the moth-soft tatters of their partial veils;
as you did the final moults of blue emperors

and common hawkers—unhooking
the lumen of each leg from its green

whiplash of reed. Your understanding
of the flesh was of the flesh

as a garment: each nymphal skin,
each *exuvia* (a word you'd discover

later, a word derived from Latin,
meaning *to strip off)* a hoard

of resinous light embossed
by evidence of an earlier life and left

hanging abandoned like a dress
too terrible to wear. Beneath the shifting

helm of leaf and bird fret you'd tipped away
the afternoon's treasures—milfoil slipping

out like a chain inside a clear limb
of poured water; spawn

in a slump in the jar's mouth until
its own weight dragged it all

at once over the lip. Within each dark
fleck inside each bright egg, the imperative,

the blind will inherited, held.
For a while.

And every flare, every slick fuse
of skin, you'd gathered

in. Dusk. Crows in the oaks. Shadows
of the world's turned-down corners.

And you, jar held out before you—Fetch-candle,
small pyre, stain of the body. So many

women inside it and no weight to the shine.

The Return of the Insect Collector, Germany, 2007

First there's the children's house of make-believe,
Some shattered dishes underneath a pine,
The playthings in the playhouse of the children.
Weep for what little things could make them glad.

ROBERT FROST

Those five one-car garages on the back road
to the school are there still, but what's gone
is the graffiti—the *fuck you* trawled in black
across the door of the garage right in the centre
of the row. Gone, the beech tree
whose leaves she watched cantering in place
high above the earth, whose bossy green breathing
she looked right into while sorting
through the gifts that seethed at the clear trap
of the attic window, where she captured,
subdued and then silenced with her killing jars
and nets the chevroned panic of the common wasp,
the wings of the admirals and clouded yellow.
Gone, the lamp-post against which someone
whose name she no longer remembers slipped
and undid the miracle of their new-sprung teeth.
The teeth she remembers: sparks like shards
of china floating on a fume of blood and spittle
inside the ladle of a mouth. Gone, the stables
of ochre brick, the hoof pick, the curry comb,
the froth-caked bit. Long gone, of course,
to the soil or the knacker, all the beautiful horses.
It was into the body of the beech tree
that a boy she thought she knew once nailed
the body of a newt. While she stood by in her body
and did nothing. However long it takes

for the terror inside a body to finally lie down
is too long. Even though for such a short time
it thrashed against the bark in a soft, dark seizure
of flame. This was the year she put away
her killing jars and nets. This was the year
she laboured to rescue everything forced to earth
by the smooth boot soles of the rain, riding
her white three-speed bicycle out into the aftermath
of every storm: hawk moths washed
from the lilac and phlox, lace wings adrift
on mirrors of standing water; and because
they twisted so viciously between her fingers,
because they greased themselves endlessly
in order to breathe, because the earth
passed through their bodies,
because they had five hearts, she returned
every single earthworm stranded in the open
on flushed expanses of tarmac to the dirt.

If she stands now where that beech once stood
there will be nothing but the slick lapping
of grass fussing silver under sunlight,
under wind. Gone, too,
that wide and waist-deep ditch
she'd always believed to be a front-line trench
running like a split seam along the edge of the wood.

Gone, the gleaming battlements of hawthorn cordoning
off the unkempt cemetery; gone, the cemetery's swing gate
with its black slatted wings and gone, of course,

the self who played there, who believed

that each mantis and cricket and wood wasp, each
ringlet, each brimstone, every common blue
coaxed or swept into the net's soft jaws
had been set free by the world, and maybe more
than once, so it might arrive, at last, into the grave
of her small hands. A girl who believed she could slip
through the noose forever. Who lay down
among the headstones and sometimes even slept
in the green cradle she made with her body in the grass.

The Lovers in Bergen-Belsen, 2010

The workers, being German, have dropped nothing—
no pop cans, no crisp packets, no cigarettes;
they have surveyed and precisely marked,

with luminous tape, the boundaries
where each long hut would once have been.
And between each hut, fresh smears

of earth where the blade of a bulldozer has muscled
off the top soil. *If you want me again,*
wrote Whitman, *look for me*

under your boot soles. Here, heartbreak
is a short walk through glass frames and crockery,
through belt buckles, cup handles, buttons and spoons.

Through clumps of hide that must have been shoes—
just leather ageing backwards, now,
towards the animal it once was. And here

in among the confetti of crushed brick
a rabbit with its life pulled so far down
into itself: the effort

to keep so still making it
so alive. But the dead are everywhere. And they remain
what they are. Out in the open, exposed on the bright

fairway the camp's main thoroughfare has now become,
two lovers are moving through the day's
green equilibrium; and to my right, through the thinned-

out pine and aspen, on bright screens
in the visitors centre, the survivors are testifying
over and over: *our lives*

consisted of hunger. Our lives consisted of cold.
Our lives consisted of hatred. I
was in a state of total estrangement from the world.

The lovers are close enough now for me to catch
the crisp architecture of their northern accents.
They are beautiful. They wear their beauty

unknowingly—all fluid
and radiance—and swing
branches of aspen, whose leaves,

with their long, flat stems, chafe
and vacillate against the slightest movement
so each leaf is a fluster of light,

so each branch is a voiceless gossip of silver.
He screamed and screamed and bit
off his own fingers. I will talk and talk

and tell this story. And the story
of this place would be the word
that defines the difference between

the expectant silence that falls when a bird,
momentarily, breaks from its singing
and the silence that holds fast forever

before a singing that will never begin.
Naked corpses and all I did was look
for my mother. The living were already dead.

The leaves of the aspen contain no silver.

Leaves are simply leaves, a green
dialect of light and water.

And the lovers have strolled without noticing
past the graves of thousands.

My Mother's Teeth

You had been held without effort and with indifference
for two full days in the soil's untidy grip before

I found them in the small round Tupperware
on the shelf above your sink. Those pale, low
battlements against which your words were born.

I say the body's ferocity to die is as real
as its ferocity to live. I remember the way
the firm seam of your lips refused every

effort we made to feed you tiny portions of food
and crushed tablets folded with honey.
I knew the undertaker had packed your throat

with gauze, caulked your mouth
into a pleasing shape and then wired your jaw
finally closed and I began dreaming

you'd been kidnapped, your mouth stuffed
with whatever was close at hand—scarf, sock,
underwear, duster—because it felt as if the world

were holding you ransom, as if a typed note
might drop through the galvanised sneer
of the letter box; that whatever the price,

I would pay it. We had cleared the paraphernalia
of your dying away: the baby food and morphine
and needles. The bed. The commode. The dressings

and tablets and fortified juices, and the oxygen
with its skeins of tubing. And because I needed
to hold them fast, in the way I held your body

fast—in mind, in the earth, with your feet
to the hills and your head to the bay and its small talk
of salt—I climbed to the lake with your teeth,

in their plastic temple, in my pocket.
You must remember how it is: the higher
you climb, the deeper the world inhabits

its essentials until there is nothing
but wind and brightness, hand in hand, heaving
through the ling and bog cotton;

and, close to the soil, the solid-green mouths
of the sundew, which never truly close, building
their sweetness out of light and rain and the rendered

bodies of insects. And I threw them in: I threw
your teeth into the silken grip of the water,
which treasures everything it is offered—even tannin

and shadow, even the dark droppings of sheep
like round buttons, even bones unbuckled
in the heather. I say the mouth

is the most dangerous kingdom of all. I say paradise
is there behind the gates of the teeth because
it is there that the tongue's nimble wand

names its hungers. And I say life means nothing
if we can't be brought willingly down and consumed
by the terrible needs in another's mouth.

There were warriors once who pried
the teeth from every defeated adversary simply
to ensure that with his mouth plundered

and his words unformed each man would walk
unarmed into the next life. Just think
what such a belief reveals about the purpose of words

in this life. But I say even in this life, sometimes,
there is no language. Only gesture. I threw them out
as far as I could. I say the living can be wounded

like water. With a final shy sound they slipped through
the skin of the lake. And I kissed them, of course,

before I threw them. Of course. Of course I held them,
gently, and with both hands, and I put them to my lips.

Ianua: Day Zero plus Twenty-One

No evidence of a body. No blood.
Just a slim hem of red on the skin of a neck
torn like felt, and strung, still, on their cord—clean
and flensed—two perfect vertebrae. Both eyes
open and each pupil a tiny snip
in the scrim of its iris. New born, perhaps;
stolen, then, soon after birth's greased flush
and spill. *Fox, then*, I think, because I have seen
how the foxes stitch the russet flames
of their appetites back and forth, searching
for a newly dropped lamb among the flock.

The rough spread fan of hillside above me.
And below, beyond the interlocking beauty
of the dry stone wall, the fields' tamed aprons
sloping down to the road. Nothing beyond this
but the ocean's vast wet sex of lunacy
and salt. Remember that moment

when Prendick, lost in the tangle
of the heat-bruised jungle on Moreau's
strange island, discovers the rabbit? That slack
headless mass before him on the narrow trail?
The sudden upsurge of dread? How we sense
his faith in benevolence coming to an end and know
he feels the held breath of every

living thing in Eden—
        why else *the luxurious ferns*
        why else that *triangular patch of glittering water*

        why else *the luminous blue of the sky*—
before hell, literally, breaks loose?

Along the horizon the heat's blue shimmy.
The tremble of a kestrel
in bright air. A few high clouds

and sunlight breaking like an animal
over the fields and I am falling to my knees
on the turf before the mouth's black flange,
on my knees before a row of teeth, each tooth
glossy and slick, each tooth pink-tinged
and translucent like the fleshed seeds
with which Persephone made
her covenant with the dead. And who
among the living doesn't want this—
not banishment, but permission?

And with a snap heard in the fingertips
each tooth breaks cleanly out from the bone
of the jaw. And who among the living
would be willing to judge me, desperate
as I am—desperate, I am desperate, I am wild
and desperate, my father

only weeks in the grave. Balanced in my hand,
like the body of a flute, the jaw's narrow strap
with its empty sockets. And how can death
not become myth: the wing
bone of a swan carved into a flute
is one of this world's oldest instruments.
Perhaps there is no better afterlife than this:
to have travelled your whole life through air
and then, after death, have breath
passing through you. And what better form
of worship can there be: to put your lips
around the sky until the dead sing?

Nothing here but the bitter liquor
of damaged grass and bone, the ransacked
jaw wrenched from its hinge. No singing.
No song. In my palm and untested
against the world for which they were born,
eight small teeth, which I fling, which I
scythe in an arc over the hillside, far out
over the bracken and the furze. Because beyond

the sheer magic of their creation—their budding
from calcium and phosphorus—no miracle in them

at all: no currency, no permission. No door.

NOTES

"DEAD DRIFT"

Stanzas twelve, thirteen, and fifteen of this poem owe a formal debt to Stephanie Brown's poem "Constellation." Brown was inspired by a line from Dan Pagis' poem "The Art of Contraction."

"ISIS ON THE MISSISSIPPI"

This poem was commissioned by *Rain Taxi Review of Books* for the fifth anniversary of the I-35W Mississippi River Bridge collapse, which occurred at 6.05 p.m. on 7 August 2007. Thirteen people died, and an additional 145 were injured, when the bridge in Minneapolis collapsed, plunging dozens of cars, lorries, and road workers into the Mississippi River. Investigations revealed that a design flaw had contributed to the collapse. The poem was read at the commemoration event in the Ruins Courtyard of Mill City Museum, Minneapolis, on 1 August 2012, and was published in the chapbook *Bridge: A Gathering*.

"THE LIONS OF CHAUVET"

Chauvet Cave, located in the Ardèche region of southern France, was discovered in 1994 by speleologists Jean-Marie Chauvet, Éliette Brunel Deschamps, and Christian Hillaire. Charcoal samples have yielded dates between 30,340 and 33,000 BP, which means that the drawings and paintings in Chauvet are almost twice as old as those in Lascaux. Over 400 images depicting at least thirteen different species, including some rarely or never found in other locations, adorn the walls of Chauvet. Rather than depicting only the familiar herbivores and "hunt" animals that tend to predominate in Palaeolithic cave art, the walls of Chauvet feature many predatory animals, such as cave lions, panthers, bears, and cave hyaenas. Access is severely restricted, and the cave has been sealed off to the public since its discovery. A replica of the cave opened in April 2015.

The filmmaker Werner Herzog visited the cave in 2010 to make the documentary *Cave of Forgotten Dreams*.

This poem is dedicated to Deborah Keenan.

"64 Unbekannte Tote: Photograph, Germany, 1970"

The house mentioned in this poem—the house I grew up in—also appears in several poems in my collection *I Wish I Had a Heart Like Yours, Walt Whitman* (University of Notre Dame Press, 2009). In fact, the following lines, which appear here in "64 Unbekannte Tote: Photograph, Germany, 1970" appear in all the earlier Bergen-Belsen poems as a device to force the reader to return, as does the speaker, to this house: "…a house that contained/at the end of the war eight hundred/sixty-nine Gypsies, Jews, and "others"—overflow/from the camp, as Stalin advanced and Hitler panicked/and prisoners were shuffled west." The repetition is used to reinforce the fact that this house and its history have haunted me all my life.

Originally built as part of a Panzer training camp (which became known as Hohne) in 1933, this house and several other buildings were taken over by the SS in early 1945 to form Bergen-Belsen Camp 2. The buildings were used, as the poems say, to contain the "overflow" from the main camp, which was less than a mile away. After liberation by the British on 15 April 1945, all the buildings in Hohne became part of a massive hospital complex for the survivors of Bergen-Belsen.

After liberation, due to starvation and an ongoing typhus epidemic, the daily death rate among survivors was in the hundreds. The 64 unidentified bodies are believed to have been Bergen-Belsen survivors who died in the hospital camp of Hohne.

"Dead Reckoning, Part III: Set and Drift"

Bee information in stanzas four through seven adapted from "Baby Clutch" by Adam Mars-Jones in *Granta 27* (Summer 1989) and the American Beekeeping Federation (http://www.abfnet.org).

"Ianua: Day Zero plus Twenty-One"

Text in italics in stanzas four and five from *The Island of Doctor Moreau* by H.G. Wells (first published in 1896).

JUDE NUTTER was born in North Yorkshire, England, and grew up near Hannover, in northern Germany. She studied printmaking at Winchester School of Art (UK) and received her MFA in poetry from the University of Oregon. Her poems have appeared in numerous national and international journals and have received over forty awards and grants, including two McKnight Fellowships, The Moth International Poetry Prize, The Larry Levis Prize, The William Matthews Prize, The Joy Harjo Poetry Award, and grants from the Elizabeth George Foundation and the National Science Foundation's Writers and Artists Program in Antarctica. Her first book-length collection, *Pictures of the Afterlife* (Salmon Poetry), winner of the Irish Listowel Prize, was published in 2002. *The Curator of Silence* (University of Notre Dame Press), her second collection, won the Ernest Sandeen Prize and was awarded the 2007 Minnesota Book Award in poetry. A third collection, *I Wish I Had a Heart Like Yours, Walt Whitman* (University of Notre Dame Press), was awarded the 2010 Minnesota Book Award in poetry and voted Poetry Book of the Year by Foreword Review, New York. She currently teaches in Minneapolis and divides her time between Minnesota and Dingle, Ireland, where she has a family home.

salmonpoetry

Cliffs of Moher, County Clare, Ireland

"Like the sea-run Steelhead salmon that thrashes upstream to its spawning ground, then instead of dying, returns to the sea—Salmon Poetry Press brings precious cargo to both Ireland and America in the poetry it publishes, then carries that select work to its readership against incalculable odds."

TESS GALLAGHER

The Salmon Bookshop
& Literary Centre

Ennistymon, County Clare, Ireland